21 POEMS FROM A 28 YEAR OLD

ROOHI ASENATH

To my Dads

Contents

Preface *vii*

Acknowledgements *ix*

1. An Ode To You 1
2. Dear Sunshine 3
3. Hello World! 5
4. Up In The Air 6
5. As The Son Of My Single Mom 7
6. The Irony Of "my Life" 8
7. The Insoluble Dilemma In Arranged Marraiges 9
8. Love Rules The Law 10
9. Night Squad 11
10. Pen Is Mightier 12
11. Profound Love 13
12. The Other Side Of Life 14
13. Sealed Love 15
14. Divine Love 17
15. Childhood Sweethearts 18
16. Magic Or Magician? 19
17. Crux 20
18. Life Or Death 21
19. Parenting Is A Process 22
20. A Journey Of Thousand Miles 23
21. The Horizons Are Calling 24

Preface

Dear Readers,

First of all, thanks for your interest and thought in picking up this book.

In December 2021, I challenged myself to write 21 poems in a span of 21 days & I managed to suceeed in the task by the end of 21 days.

This book is a collection of my random thoughts and writings that I penned down taking inspiration from people & stories around me.

Love & Peace,

Roohi Asenath

Acknowledgements

Many thanks

to

Vaishu, the one who read my first drafts.

Devi, the one who gave me the title of this book.

1. An ode to you

All these days, my Love
I lived by manic ideology.
I was a mere number,
A faceless static lost in the thoughts of peripheral world.
When you happened, my Love
You turned to be my epiphany.
You breathed new life into me.
A life beaming with scintillating aura
that I always longed for in this chaotic world.
You held my hand tight
You lead my healing
You groomed my metaphysics
You showed my forevers
You reassured me countless times
that it's gonna be alright.
Thanks to you,
a girl who once was bellowed,
is now radiant and mellowed.
A girl who once was rebellious
is now up for her remedials.
A girl who once was a worrywart,
is now everybody's sweet heart.
A girl who once was cramped by her traumas and tantrums
is now tranquil radiating her colors of spectrum.
All these came to pass

because behind every successful woman
a man there was!

2. Dear Sunshine

Dear Sunshine,
Where are you?
I wish I could see you everyday
Because you give me the rays of hope
Are the days really numbered?
When I look at the horizon
I yearn!
I yearn to be the sea
Be it rainy or windy
Sunny or stormy
My wish to see you never fades away
Why do I yearn?
Why do I yearn so much?
I couldn't find the reason
May be you could!
Will you find it out for my sake?
Dear Sunshine,
Will you ever get the message that wanders in my heart?
Should I seek the help of nature?
Should I seek the help of heaven?
Should I seek the help of almighty?
Whom should I cling on to?
All my questions remain a boomerang.
While all the answers remain with you.
Dear Sunshine,

It's not that I want you.
Rather, I need you!
Today & forever!

3. Hello world!

It was the night that made me think of
stars and galaxies,
oceans and seas,
rain and rainbow,
coffee and croissants,
deserts and dinosaurs,
crop circles and cappuccino,
aliens and aurora,
peacocks and periwinkles,
sun and moon,
mountains and mud.
Of all these mysterious beauties of the world,
the cosmos still chose to create
a mystery that stood out the times.
Hello Human race!
May I ask you how you managed to land up here?

4. Up in the air

She is just up in the air, finally!
Once there were war flights,
And she survived.
Once it was raining cats and dogs,
And she survived.
Once there was scorching heat,
And she survived.
Once there were hailing stones,
And she survived.
Once there was a monstrous storm,
And she survived.
She is just up in the air, finally!
Leaving behind all those people on the land who were not ready to come out of their comfort zones.
Leaving behind all those people on the land who told her a million times that it is beyond her strength to be flying.
Leaving behind all those people on the land who tried their best to break her dreams.
Leaving behind all those people on the land who mocked her in every possible way of her broken wings.
Yes, her wounds could be deep.
But the depth of her want surpasses all.

5. As the son of my single mom

I've held my heart high
when she needed me.
I've held my heart high
when she smiled at me.
I've held my heart high
when she questioned me.
I've held my heart high
when she cheered me.
I've held my heart high
when she chastised me.
I've held my heart high
when she loved me.
I've held my heart high
when she left me.
Because I know
that somewhere in the heavens,
she is still proud
that her son made it to the finish line
even without his mother on his side.
The tears of my mother wished me
on my graduation day
And I've held my heart high
one more time for my mum
when it rained.

6. The irony of "My life"

When I sit back & contemplate on life, it's just so damn ironical.
I call it "My life". Yet, I didn't get to choose my parents.
I call it " My life". Yet, I didn't get to choose my birthplace.
I call it "My life". Yet, I didn't get to choose my name.
I call it "My life". Yet, I didn't get to choose my skin colour.
I call it " My life". Yet, I didn't get to choose my being.
Isn't that strange?
And here's to the worst part!
Many of us think that we are way beyond the sky
Not even realizing that we are just puppets in the hands of supremacy.

7. The insoluble dilemma in arranged marraiges

Are you melody or melancholy?
Are you sunshine or moon light?
Are you yin or yang?
Are you horizon or seashore?
Are you rainbow or thunder?
Are you mermaid or unicorn?
Are you sugar or sugar-coated?
Are you kombucha or kunafa?
Are you summer or winter?
Are you autumn or spring?
Endless questions that keep popping up in my mind before saying yes.

8. Love rules the law

Yes, not having food is tough.
But it's tougher to not have anybody to ask you if you had anything.
Yes, not having money is tough.
But it's tougher to not have anybody to ask you if you will need any money.
Yes, not having a shelter is tough.
But it's tougher to not have anybody to ask you if you will need any space.
Yes, not having a job is tough.
But it's tougher to not have anybody to wish you the best for the interviews.
Yes, not getting to smile is tough.
But it's tougher to not have anybody wipe the tears off your cheeks at 3 A.M.
Yes, not getting sunshine is tough.
But it's tougher to not have anybody run behind you to remind you of the umbrella when it rains.

9. Night squad

Night is a window
that opens your past present & future
that opens your smile, tear & trauma
that opens your fear, love & hate
that opens your mind, soul & heart altogether!

10. Pen is mightier

Someone asked me what it is to be a writer.
Let me tell you, my friend!
A writer is an ocean.
A writer is a pen pal.
A writer need not abide by the rules of a language.
A writer is a mistake.
A writer is an exception.
She could be the sunrise & sunset of someone's life.
She could be a boomerang or a doppelganger.
She can penetrate your souls.
She can occupy your mind & heart.
She can console you.
She can bother you.
She can question your existence & purpose.
She can question your guilt & shame.
She can parent you.
She can play with your inner child.
She can do a lot more than others who fail to notice you.
So, the next time you open a book to read, don't forget to say Hi to your new friend who will accompany you throughout your read or maybe even longer than expected.

11. Profound love

She asked him for a flower
Yet expected him to present her a bouquet.
He walked in, held her hands & opened the windows of her room.
Pointing out to the once barren land,
he said: Here's your garden, Daughter!

12. The other side of life

Stop!
Stop asking me for my score & ranks.
Stop asking me if I have attained puberty.
Stop asking me if I am getting married.
Stop asking me if I am gonna have a baby
Stop asking me if I am earning enough
Stop it!
Just stop it!
If you can
Ask me if I am happy
Ask me if I am peaceful
Ask me if I am healthy
Ask me if I am leading a purposeful life
Because these really count for the essentials.

13. Sealed love

What will I do with those unsent letters, Abdul?
Now that they are sealed
And forbidden for anybody to read!
I can't read them because I wasn't the same who wrote them years ago!
I should have posted them to you, Abu!
When you were still alive,
I should have posted them to you!
I should have given you the chance to breath my words
Soaked in my love & tears before we parted ways.
I couldn't stop my muhurtham because I chose to live.
But you managed to stop your Nikkah because you chose to leave.
Our destiny is hitting me hard!
Why did we meet?
Why did we like each other?
Why did we fall in love?
Why did we take birth in a caste obsessed society?
My head stumbles when I keep asking these endless questions to myself.
Well, you know that my love & peace remains with you.
It's just that my flesh is separated from yours.
Insha Allah! Let's meet on the other side soon, Abu!
To fall in love one more time,
to smile & cry together one more time,
in a safer & better place.

And when I come there, I am bringing my letters to you in mint condition,
I promise!
Love,
Meenakshi Abdul

14. Divine love

When I miss the one I love
I look at the sky & stars.
And tell myself:
"We are at least under the same sky".
We need not meet each other
We need not hear each other
We need not exchange letters
But we know.
We know that we like each other.
We know that we respect each other.
We know that we care for each other.
We know that we miss each other.
Yet,
We also know that we can't be together.
Let it be.
Not all love walk down the aisle.
In fact, the ones that don't succeed attain divinity.

15. Childhood sweethearts

To the moon & back I feel
From head over heels I fell
To the world and you I tell
My raw & random thoughts so real
Every night over my cup of coffee
Listening to the 90's songs on Murphy
Reliving our small fights over the toffee
Sharing the geometry box so glossy
Getting excited for tiny little pleasures
That we sit back today & talk for hours
Our times together are good old treasures
That hardly knows any measures
From floppy disks to pen drives
From comic books to kindle
From desktops to laptops
From letters to e-mails
We have seen the transitions together
Dear childhood sweetheart,
I am up for our major transition today
From mates to partners
From friends to family
From neighbors to spouses
From peers to parents
Forget not to write a reply letter to me
If you too keep thinking about me

16. Magic or Magician?

The stars lose their mind
When they see you smile
The clouds forget to rain
When they see you weep
The birds stop to chirp
When they hear you sing
The flowers choose not to bloom
When they see you dance
My heart stops to beat
Just by hearing your name!
Reveal it to me!
Are you magic? or magician?

17. Crux

He said:

"Don't think too much about me. I was just a chapter in your book."

I said:

"Yes, indeed. But what you know not is that the crux of the story revolves around that particular chapter. Holding on is hard. Letting go is harder, my friend!"

18. Life or Death

The sky changes its colour
When he wants to convey his message to the world.
When he is happy, he shows up in red.
When he is sad, he shows up in grey.
When he is hopeful, he shows up in vibgyor.
When he is talking, he shows up in white.
Whereas, we, the humans,
We show up just two colours.
We are either on the path of life or the path of death.
It is either dark or light.
There is no in-between!

19. Parenting is a process

What is mindful parenting?
When your inner child doesn't affect your child
And when the adult in you penetrates through the barriers
To see the adult in your child.
That pretty much sums up everything!
Heal, Heal Dear One!
Before you find your family
So that your child need not deal with your traumas!
Keep pressing, one day at a time!

20. A journey of thousand miles

I knew her life in a second
When she asked me a question that nobody had ever asked me:
"By the way, how does it feel to be loved?"
And that's the day I decided
To show her what it means.
From friends to spouses,
From concerns to care,
From affection to love,
It's a mellifluous journey.

21. The horizons are calling

Pay heed, Oh woman!
The one who is fond of purple
And the one who hates the darkness!
It's time to paint your life with a spectrum of hues,
For your generations will know that a transcendentalist existed in their lineage!
You, the woman of forbearance, strength & hope
Rejoice & rejoice, the woman of endurance!
The horizons are calling you today
Because they saw you chasing the sunshine every single day.

Printed by Libri Plureos GmbH in Hamburg,
Germany